contents

Christmas comes but once a year, but there's a lot of planning and thought that is done long before the festivities begin. This book is for those of us who like to make something a little different, it might be for the family Christmas get-together, or it might be for gifts for special friends, either way, you're going to find some wonderful and unique ideas here in these pages.

Pamela Clark

Food Director

This is the prettiest Christmas book you'll ever see. It's not the usual Christmas cookbook – there are no recipes for turkey or ham. Instead it's full of clever recipes for small festive food – little biscuits and cakes, puddings and tarts. There are also butters, jams and chutneys – wonderful Christmas presents.

gingerbread christmas trees

The trees will keep for several weeks in airtight containers. You will have a lot of royal icing left over, use it for making snow on the trees if you like, or halve the recipe.

3 cups (450g) self-raising flour
¾ cup (165g) firmly packed
   brown sugar
1 tablespoon ground ginger
1 teaspoon ground cinnamon
1 teaspoon ground nutmeg
½ teaspoon ground clove
185g butter, chopped coarsely
¾ cup (270g) golden syrup
1 egg
silver cachous
1 tablespoon icing sugar
royal icing
1 egg white
1½ cups (240g) pure icing sugar

1 Process flour, brown sugar, spices and butter until crumbly. Add golden syrup and egg; process until combined. Knead dough on floured surface until smooth. Cover; refrigerate 1 hour.
2 Divide dough in half; roll each half between sheets of baking paper to 5mm thickness. Refrigerate 30 minutes.
3 Preheat oven to 180°C/160°C fan-forced. Line oven trays with baking paper.
4 Cut twelve 3cm, twelve 5cm, twelve 6cm, twelve 7cm, twelve 8cm, and twelve 9cm stars from dough; transfer stars to trays. You will need to reroll the dough several times to get the correct number of stars.
5 Bake 3cm, 5cm and 6cm stars about 10 minutes and remaining stars about 12 minutes.
6 Meanwhile, make royal icing.
7 Assemble trees by joining two 9cm stars, two 8cm stars, two 7cm stars, two 6cm stars, two 5cm stars and two 3cm stars with a little royal icing between each star. Decorate trees by joining cachous to stars with a tiny dot of royal icing. Dust trees with sifted icing sugar.

royal icing Sift icing sugar through fine sieve. Beat egg white until foamy in small bowl with electric mixer; beat in icing sugar a tablespoon at a time.

makes 6

300g toasted marshmallows with coconut, chopped coarsely
½ cup (40g) flaked almonds, roasted
4 slices glacé pineapple (125g), chopped coarsely
½ cup (125g) coarsely chopped glacé peaches
½ cup (100g) coarsely chopped glacé citron
450g white eating chocolate, melted

1 Grease 19cm x 29cm slice pan; line base and two long sides with baking paper, extending paper 5cm over long sides.
2 Combine marshmallows, nuts and fruit in large bowl. Working quickly, stir in chocolate; spread mixture into pan, push mixture down firmly to flatten.
3 Refrigerate rocky road until set before cutting into squares.

makes 35

jewelled rocky road

stained glass christmas trees

1 vanilla bean
250g butter, softened
¾ cup (165g) caster sugar
1 egg
1 tablespoon water
2¼ cups (335g) plain flour
90g individually wrapped
    sugar-free fruit drops,
    assorted colours

1 Split vanilla bean in half lengthways; scrape seeds into medium bowl with butter, sugar, egg and the water. Beat with an electric mixer until combined. Stir in sifted flour, in two batches. Knead dough on floured surface until smooth. Cover; refrigerate 30 minutes.

2 Preheat oven to 180°C/160°C fan-forced. Line two oven trays with baking paper.

3 Using a rolling pin, gently tap wrapped lollies to crush them slightly. Unwrap lollies, separate by colour into small bowls. (See page 108.)

4 Roll dough between sheets of baking paper to 4mm thickness. Cut shapes from dough using 8cm long Christmas tree cutter; place cookies on oven trays. Use a 4cm long Christmas tree or 1.5cm star cutter to cut out the centre of each tree to make windows. Using a skewer, make a small hole in the top of each tree for threading through ribbon (see page 108).

5 Bake trees 7 minutes. Remove trays from oven; fill each window in trees with a few of the same-coloured lollies (see page 108). Bake a further 5 minutes or until browned lightly. Cool trees on trays.

makes 32

sweet shortbread spirals

½ cup (110g) caster sugar
100g cold butter, chopped
  coarsely
1¼ cups (185g) plain flour
1 egg yolk
1 tablespoon milk
1½ cups (400g) cranberry &
  apple fruit mince (see page 78)
¼ cup (80g) apricot jam,
  warmed, sieved

1 Process sugar, butter and sifted flour until crumbly. Add egg yolk and milk; process until combined. Knead dough on floured surface until smooth. Cover; refrigerate 30 minutes.
2 Meanwhile, process fruit mince until chopped finely.
3 Roll dough between two sheets of baking paper to 25cm x 30cm. Spread fruit mince evenly over rectangle, leaving 1cm border. Using paper as a guide, roll rectangle tightly from short side to enclose filling. Wrap roll in baking paper; refrigerate 30 minutes.
4 Preheat oven to 160°C/140°C fan-forced. Grease two oven trays; line with baking paper.
5 Trim edges of roll; cut roll into 1cm slices. Place slices, cut-side up, onto oven trays.
6 Bake spirals about 20 minutes. Cool on tray; brush tops with warm jam.

makes 25

3 egg whites
2 tablespoons caster sugar
pink food colouring
1 cup (120g) almond meal
1¼ cups (200g) icing sugar
2 tablespoons icing sugar, extra
white chocolate ganache
180g white eating chocolate,
   chopped coarsely
⅓ cup (80ml) cream

1 Preheat oven to 150°C/130°C fan-forced. Grease two oven trays; line with baking paper.
2 Beat egg whites in small bowl with electric mixer until soft peaks form. Gradually add caster sugar, beating until dissolved between additions. Tint with food colouring.
3 Transfer mixture to large bowl; fold in almond meal and sifted icing sugar. Spoon mixture into piping bag fitted with 1.5cm plain tube. Pipe macaroons onto trays 4cm apart; dust macaroons with extra sifted icing sugar. Stand 15 minutes; bake about 20 minutes.
4 Meanwhile, make white chocolate ganache.
5 Cool macaroons on trays. Sandwich macaroons with ganache.

white chocolate ganache Stir chocolate and cream in small saucepan over low heat until smooth. Refrigerate 1 hour or until ganache is spreadable.

makes 16

parisian macaroons

choc-nut brandy snap wafers

60g butter
¼ cup (55g) firmly packed
  brown sugar
2 tablespoons golden syrup
1 teaspoon ground cinnamon
½ cup (75g) plain flour
½ cup (70g) unroasted
  hazelnuts, chopped coarsely
½ cup (70g) unsalted pistachios,
  chopped coarsely
100g dark eating chocolate,
  chopped finely

1 Preheat oven to 180°C/160°C fan-forced. Grease two oven trays; line with baking paper.
2 Stir butter, sugar, golden syrup and cinnamon in small saucepan over low heat until butter has melted. Remove from heat; stir in flour.
3 Working quickly, spread four 12cm squares of mixture about 3cm apart onto trays. Bake 2 minutes; sprinkle with combined nuts. Bake about 5 minutes or until brandy snaps bubble and become golden brown.
4 Remove from oven; sprinkle with chocolate immediately. Cool on trays. Cut into squares.

makes 16

jam wreaths

250g butter, softened
1 teaspoon finely grated
   lemon rind
⅓ cup (75g) caster sugar
2 cups (300g) plain flour
½ cup (100g) rice flour
½ cup (160g) raspberry jam
1 tablespoon caster sugar, extra

1 Beat butter, rind and sugar in medium bowl with electric mixer until combined. Stir in sifted flours, in two batches. Knead dough on floured surface until smooth. Cover; refrigerate 30 minutes.

2 Preheat oven to 180°C/160°C fan-forced. Line two oven trays with baking paper.

3 Roll three-quarters of the dough between sheets of baking paper to 4mm thickness; cut twenty 6.5cm rounds from dough. Place rounds 4cm apart on oven trays.

4 Roll remaining dough between sheets of baking paper to 4mm thickness. Using a 4cm holly cutter, cut out leaves from dough.

5 Brush edge of each round of dough lightly with water; arrange leaves, overlapping slightly, around edge (see page 108). Sprinkle leaves lightly with extra sugar. Spoon jam into the centre of each wreath (see page 109).

6 Bake wreaths about 20 minutes. Cool on trays.

makes 20

125g butter, softened
¾ cup (165g) caster sugar
1 egg
1¾ cups (255g) plain flour
⅓ cup (50g) self-raising flour
2 tablespoons coarse white
  sugar crystals (see glossary)
red ribbon
lemon royal icing
2 cups (320g) pure icing sugar
1 egg white
2 teaspoons lemon juice

1 Beat butter, caster sugar and egg in small bowl with electric mixer until light and fluffy. Stir in sifted flours in two batches. Knead dough on floured surface until smooth. Cover; refrigerate 30 minutes.
2 Preheat oven to 180°C/160°C fan-forced. Line two oven trays with baking paper.
3 Roll dough between sheets of baking paper to 5mm thickness. Cut twenty 8cm x 11cm angel shapes from dough; cut two 1.5cm moon shapes from each shoulder of angel shapes for threading ribbon. Place angels on oven trays.
4 Bake angels about 12 minutes. Cool cookies on trays.
5 Meanwhile, make lemon royal icing.
6 Spread angels with icing; sprinkle with sugar crystals. Set icing at room temperature; thread ribbon through holes.

lemon royal icing Sift icing sugar through fine sieve. Beat egg white until foamy in small bowl with electric mixer; beat in icing sugar a tablespoon at a time. Stir in juice.

makes 20

angel gift tags

Store these more-ish cookies in an airtight container for up to 4 weeks – or wrap for a lovely gift.

1 cup (140g) coarsely chopped seeded dates
2 tablespoons golden syrup
2 tablespoons water
¼ teaspoon bicarbonate soda
1 teaspoon finely grated orange rind
1¾ cups (255g) plain flour
¾ cup (165g) caster sugar
100g butter, chopped coarsely
1 egg
¼ cup (40g) icing sugar

1 Preheat oven to 180°C/160°C fan-forced. Grease two oven trays; line with baking paper.
2 Combine dates, syrup and the water in small saucepan; bring to the boil. Remove from heat, stir in soda and rind; stand 5 minutes. Process date mixture until almost smooth; cool.
3 Add flour, caster sugar, butter and egg to processor. Process until ingredients come together. Refrigerate mixture 30 minutes.
4 Roll heaped teaspoons of mixture into balls; flatten slightly. Place about 3cm apart on oven trays.
5 Bake cookies about 15 minutes. Cool on trays; toss in sifted icing sugar.

makes 30

sticky date cookies

white christmas mud cakes

125g butter, chopped coarsely
125g white eating chocolate, chopped coarsely
⅔ cup (150g) caster sugar
⅔ cup (160ml) milk
¾ cup (105g) plain flour
¼ cup (35g) self-raising flour
2 eggs
2 tablespoons Cointreau
60g white eating chocolate melted, extra
1 tablespoon icing sugar
white christmas
120g white eating chocolate, chopped coarsely
2 teaspoons vegetable oil
¾ cup (30g) rice bubbles
100g marshmallows with toasted coconut, chopped finely
¼ cup (35g) coarsely chopped unsalted pistachios
¼ cup (35g) coarsely chopped dried cranberries
¼ cup (60g) finely chopped glacé peaches

1 Preheat oven to 160°C/140°C fan-forced. Grease eight ¾-cup (180ml) pudding moulds.
2 Stir butter, chocolate, caster sugar and milk in medium saucepan over low heat until smooth. Transfer to medium bowl; cool 10 minutes. Whisk in sifted flours, then eggs. Spoon cake mixture into moulds; place on oven tray.
3 Bake cakes about 30 minutes; drizzle cakes with liqueur. Turn hot cakes, still in their moulds, upside down onto baking-paper-lined tray; stand overnight.
4 Cut four 20cm circles from baking paper; cut circles in half. Roll each half into a tight cone. Staple or tape cones to hold their shape. (See page 112.)
5 Make white christmas.
6 Push spoonfuls of white christmas firmly into cones. Stand each cone upright in a tall narrow glass. Refrigerate cones about 1 hour or until set.

7 Remove cakes from moulds. Trim tops of cakes to make flat; turn upside down onto tray. Remove white christmas cones from paper; secure cones to each cake with a little of the extra chocolate. Refrigerate 10 minutes. Serve mud cakes dusted with sifted icing sugar.
white christmas Stir chocolate and oil in small saucepan over low heat until smooth. Combine rice bubbles, marshmallow, nuts and fruit in medium bowl; stir in melted chocolate mixture.

makes 8

rich chocolate christmas cakes

Buy 200g muscatels for these cakes, use one-third in the cake mixture and the rest for decorating.

1 cup (170g) seeded prunes
1 cup (140g) seeded dried dates
1 cup (150g) raisins
½ cup (75g) muscatels
1 cup (200g) dried figs
5 (100g) glacé orange slices
1½ cups (375ml) Irish whiskey
1½ cups (330g) firmly packed
    dark brown sugar
185g butter, softened
3 eggs
½ cup (50g) hazelnut meal
1½ cups (225g) plain flour
2 tablespoons cocoa powder
1 teaspoon mixed spice
½ teaspoon ground nutmeg
½ teaspoon bicarbonate of soda
150g dark eating chocolate,
    chopped finely
¼ cup (60ml) water
2 tablespoons cocoa powder,
    extra
1 cup (150g) muscatels, extra

1 Chop all fruit finely. Combine fruit and ¾ cup of the whiskey in large bowl, cover with plastic wrap; stand overnight.
2 Preheat oven to 120°C/100°C fan-forced. Line eight deep 8cm-round cake tins with two thicknesses of baking paper, extending paper 5cm above sides of tins.
3 Stir remaining whiskey and ¾ cup of the sugar in small saucepan over heat until sugar dissolves; bring to the boil. Remove from heat; cool syrup 20 minutes.
4 Meanwhile, beat butter and remaining sugar in small bowl with electric mixer until combined; beat in eggs, one at a time. Add butter mixture to fruit mixture; mix well. Mix in meal, sifted dry ingredients, chocolate and ½ cup of the cooled syrup. Spread mixture into tins.
5 Bake cakes about 1¾ hours.

6 Bring remaining syrup and the water to the boil in small saucepan; boil for 3 minutes or until thickened slightly. Brush hot cakes with half of the hot syrup, cover cakes with foil; cool in tins.
7 Divide reserved muscatels into eight small bunches; place bunches in remaining syrup. Stand in syrup until cool, drain.
8 Dust cakes with extra sifted cocoa, top with muscatel bunches.

makes 8

chocolate mousse snowballs

3 eggs
2½ tablespoons firmly packed
  brown sugar
240g dark eating chocolate,
  melted
⅔ cup (160ml) thick cream
  (48% fat)
2 tablespoons Cointreau
360g white eating chocolate,
  chopped coarsely
2 teaspoons vegetable oil
2 cups (100g) flaked coconut

1 Preheat oven to 180°C/160°C fan-forced. Grease deep 15cm-round cake pan; line base and side with baking paper.

2 Beat eggs and sugar in medium bowl with electric mixer until thick and creamy. Beat in cooled dark chocolate.

3 Fold in combined cream and liqueur; pour mixture into pan. Place pan in baking dish; pour enough boiling water into dish to come halfway up side of pan.

4 Bake cake 30 minutes. Cover loosely with foil; bake further 25 minutes. Cool cake in pan; refrigerate overnight.

5 Divide cake evenly into six wedges. Roll each wedge of cake into a ball, place on fine wire rack. Freeze balls about 1 hour or until firm.

6 Stir white chocolate and oil in small saucepan over low heat until smooth; cool 5 minutes. Spoon white chocolate mixture over balls to coat; freeze 5 minutes. Coat balls again with white chocolate mixture; roll in coconut. Refrigerate 20 minutes before serving in dessert dishes.

makes 6

glacé fruit cakes with ginger syrup

¾ cup (105g) slivered almonds
90g butter, softened
2 teaspoons finely grated
   lemon rind
¾ cup (165g) caster sugar
2 eggs
¾ cup (110g) plain flour
½ cup (75g) self-raising flour
⅓ cup (80ml) milk
4 slices glacé pineapple (125g),
   chopped coarsely
⅓ cup (70g) red glacé cherries,
   halved
⅓ cup (70g) green glacé
   cherries, halved
⅓ cup (75g) coarsely chopped
   glacé ginger
½ cup (70g) slivered almonds,
   extra
ginger syrup
¾ cup (180ml) water
¾ cup (165g) caster sugar
2cm piece fresh ginger (10g),
   grated

1 Preheat oven to 170°C/150°C fan-forced. Grease 12-hole (⅓-cup/80ml) muffin pan; line bases with baking paper.
2 Sprinkle nuts into pan holes.
3 Beat butter, rind and sugar in small bowl with electric mixer until light and fluffy. Beat in eggs one at a time.
4 Transfer mixture to medium bowl; stir in sifted flours, milk, fruit and extra nuts. Spread mixture into pan holes.
5 Bake cakes about 25 minutes.
6 Meanwhile, make ginger syrup.
7 Remove cakes from oven; pour hot syrup over hot cakes in pan. Cool cakes in pan.
8 Serve cakes warm or cold with cream or ice-cream.
ginger syrup Stir ingredients in small saucepan over heat, without boiling, until sugar dissolves; bring to the boil. Reduce heat; simmer, uncovered, without stirring, about 5 minutes or until syrup thickens slightly.

makes 12

4½ cups (1.1kg) cranberry &
   apple fruit mince (see page 78)
185g butter, chopped coarsely
¾ cup (165g) firmly packed
   brown sugar
⅓ cup (80ml) bourbon whiskey
⅓ cup (80ml) water
2 teaspoons finely grated
   orange rind
1 teaspoon finely grated
   lemon rind
1 tablespoon treacle
3 eggs
1¼ cups (185g) plain flour
¼ cup (35g) self-raising flour
½ teaspoon bicarbonate of soda
500g ready-made white icing
100g ready-made almond icing
1 cup (160g) icing sugar
1 egg white

1 Combine fruit mince, butter, brown sugar, whiskey and the water in large saucepan, stir over heat until butter is melted and sugar dissolved; bring to the boil. Remove from heat; transfer to large heatproof bowl. Cool.
2 Preheat oven to 150°C/130°C fan-forced. Line 22 holes of two 12-hole (⅓-cup/80ml) muffin pans with paper cases.
3 Stir rinds, treacle and eggs into fruit mixture, then sifted flours and soda. Spoon mixture into paper cases.
4 Bake cakes about 40 minutes. Cover; cool in pan overnight.
5 Trim top of each cake to make it flat. Knead white icing and almond icing together on bench dusted with some of the sifted icing sugar until smooth. Roll three-quarters of the icing to 5mm thickness. Cut 22 x 6.5cm rounds from icing; cut a 2cm round from centre of each round.

6 Brush top of each cake with egg white; top with icing rounds. Roll remaining icing on bench dusted with more sifted icing sugar to 3mm thickness. Cut out 22 stars using a 4cm cutter and 44 stars using a 1.5cm cutter. Decorate cakes with stars by brushing each with a little egg white to secure in position.

makes 22

christmas star cakes

celebration christmas cakes

Macerate the fruit and liqueur for up to a month if time permits. Stir the fruit mixture each week.

3 cups (500g) sultanas
1¾ cups (300g) raisins
1¾ cups (300g) seeded dried dates
1 cup (150g) dried currants
¼ cup (40g) candied orange
⅔ cup (130g) red glacé cherries
¼ cup (55g) glacé ginger
¼ cup (60g) dried apricots
½ cup (125ml) Grand Marnier
250g butter, softened
1 cup (220g) firmly packed brown sugar
5 eggs
1½ cups (225g) plain flour
⅓ cup (50g) self-raising flour
1 teaspoon mixed spice
2 tablespoons Grand Marnier, extra
1kg ready-made white icing
1 egg white
½ cup (80g) icing sugar
20cm-square cake board
60g jar silver cachous
1.5m silver ribbon

1 Chop all fruit the same size as sultanas. Combine fruit and liqueur in large bowl; cover with plastic wrap, stand overnight.
2 Preheat oven to 150°C/130°C fan-forced. Line two deep 15cm-square cake pans with three thicknesses of baking paper, extending paper 5cm above sides of pans.
3 Beat butter and brown sugar in small bowl with electric mixer until combined; beat in eggs one at a time. Add butter mixture to fruit mixture; mix well. Mix in sifted flours and spice; divide mixture between pans.
4 Bake cakes about 2 hours. Brush hot cakes with extra liqueur. Cover hot cakes in pan tightly with foil, turn upside down, on bench; cool overnight.
5 Trim top of one cake if necessary to make it flat. Mix a walnut-sized piece of white icing with enough cold boiled water to make a sticky paste. Spread half of this mixture into the centre of a sheet of baking paper about 5cm larger than the cake; position cake flat-side down on paper. Using a metal spatula and small pieces of white icing, patch any holes in the cake.

6 Brush egg white evenly over cake. Knead half of the remaining white icing on surface dusted with sifted icing sugar until smooth; roll to 7mm thickness. Lift icing onto cake with rolling pin, smoothing icing over cake with hands dusted with icing sugar. Cut excess icing away from base of cake.
7 Mix icing scraps with cold boiled water to make a sticky paste. Spread half of paste in centre of cake board; centre cake on board. Cut away excess baking paper around base of cake.
8 Gently push a 6cm bell-shaped cutter three-quarters of the way into icing. Using a small sharp knife carefully remove about half of the icing inside the bell shape. Carefully pull cutter out of icing. Push cachous gently into icing to fill bell. Secure half the ribbon around cake using pins. Repeat with second cake.

makes 2

chocolate panettone

¾ cup (180ml) warm milk
1 teaspoon caster sugar
2 x 7g sachets (1 tablespoon)
  dried yeast
2¼ cups (335g) plain flour
⅓ cup (35g) cocoa powder
¼ cup (55g) caster sugar, extra
1 teaspoon coarse cooking salt
1 teaspoon vanilla extract
50g butter, softened
2 eggs
2 egg yolks
½ cup (90g) raisins
⅓ cup (45g) coarsely chopped
  seeded dried dates
½ cup (95g) dark Choc Bits
1 egg, extra
2 teaspoons icing sugar

1 Combine milk, caster sugar and yeast in medium jug. Cover; stand in warm place about 10 minutes or until frothy.
2 Sift flour, cocoa, extra caster sugar and salt into large bowl; stir in yeast mixture, extract, butter, eggs, yolks, fruit and Choc Bits. Knead dough on floured surface about 10 minutes or until elastic. Place dough in greased large bowl. Cover; stand in warm place about 1 hour or until doubled in size.
3 Preheat oven to 200°C/180°C fan-forced. Line 6-hole texas (¾-cup/180ml) muffin pan with paper cases. To make your own paper cases, cut six 15cm squares from baking paper. Cut six 15cm squares from standard photocopier paper. Line pan first with paper, then with baking paper set at a different angle.

4 Knead dough on floured surface about 10 minutes or until dough loses its stickiness. Divide dough into six equal portions and press into pan holes. Cover loosely, stand in warm place about 30 minutes or until doubled in size. Brush panettone with extra egg.
5 Bake panettone 25 minutes. Stand in pan 5 minutes; turn top-side up, onto wire rack to cool. Dust with sifted icing sugar.

makes 6

mini chocolate yule logs

We baked these cakes in eight 170g passionfruit pulp cans (5.5cm diameter, 8.5cm tall). Open the cans with an opener that removes the rims from cans (ring-pull cans are not suitable). Freeze pulp for another use. Remove and discard the paper label from cans, then wash and dry the cans well.

1 cup (150g) seeded dried dates
1 cup (190g) seeded prunes
1 cup (200g) dried figs
1 cup (140g) brazil nuts
2 eggs
½ cup (110g) firmly packed
   brown sugar
1 tablespoon dark rum
100g butter, melted
⅓ cup (50g) plain four
¼ cup (35g) self-raising flour
100g dark eating chocolate,
   melted
1 tablespoon icing sugar
chocolate ganache
200g dark eating chocolate,
   chopped coarsely
½ cup (125ml) cream

1 Preheat oven to 150°C/130°C fan-forced. Grease cans; line with baking paper.
2 Chop fruit and nuts finely; combine in large bowl.
3 Beat eggs and sugar in small bowl with electric mixer until thick and creamy. Add rum, butter and sifted flours; beat until combined. Stir egg mixture into fruit mixture. Push mixture firmly into cans; place cans on oven tray.
4 Bake cakes about 30 minutes. Turn top-side up onto wire rack to cool.
5 Meanwhile, make chocolate ganache.
6 Line tray with baking paper; spread chocolate into 26cm square. Refrigerate until set.
7 Cut four of the cakes in half crossways. Sandwich one large cake and one half of cake, end-to-end, together with ganache (see page 109). Repeat with remaining large cakes and three of the halves of remaining cake to make four logs.

8 Trim bottom corner from each of the remaining cake halves (see page 109). Attach to sides of long cakes with ganache (see page 109).
9 Place logs on boards or plates; spread all over with ganache. Break chocolate into small pieces, gently push into ganache. Refrigerate until set. Serve dusted with sifted icing sugar.
chocolate ganache Stir ingredients in small bowl over small saucepan of simmering water until smooth. Refrigerate about 30 minutes, stirring occasionally, until spreadable.

makes 4

two 14cm x 20cm sponge
  cakes (400g)
1½ cups (375ml) boiling water
85g packet raspberry
  jelly crystals
½ cup (160g) jellied
  cranberry sauce
500g frozen mixed berries
1 teaspoon finely grated
  orange rind
1 tablespoon icing sugar

1 Cut twelve 2cm-thick slices
from sponges; halve slices
crossways. Cut four 2cm rounds
and four 7cm rounds from
remaining cake; trim rounds to
2cm thickness (see page 110).
2 Line four 1½-cup (375ml)
pudding moulds with plastic
wrap, leaving some wrap
hanging over the edge of the
moulds. Place small sponge
rounds into each mould. Place
sponge strips around the inside
of each mould (see page 110).
3 Pour the boiling water into
a large heatproof jug; stir in
jelly crystals and cranberry
sauce until clear. Stir in berries;
strain, reserve berries and
liquid separately.

4 Divide berries among moulds;
pressing down firmly. Spoon
1 tablespoon of the reserved
liquid over each pudding. Top
puddings with large sponge
rounds. Spoon another
tablespoon of liquid over each
pudding. Cover puddings
with overhanging plastic wrap.
Refrigerate 3 hours or overnight.
5 Bring remaining liquid to the
boil in small saucepan. Reduce
heat, simmer about 5 minutes or
until thickened slightly. Cool.
6 Turn puddings onto plates;
brush with the liquid. Serve
topped with extra frozen or fresh
mixed berries, dusted with sifted
icing sugar. Serve with cream.

makes 4

baby berry puddings

chocolate panettone puds

1 cup (270g) cranberry & apple
   fruit mince (see page 78)
2 x 170g chocolate panettone
   (see page 37)
custard
1 cup (250ml) cream
¾ cup (180ml) milk
2 tablespoons caster sugar
½ teaspoon vanilla extract
2 eggs

1 Preheat oven to 170°C/150°C
fan-forced. Grease six 1¼-cup
(310ml) ovenproof teacups.
2 Make custard.
3 Cut panettone in half
lengthways. Cut halves into
thick slices.
4 Layer panettone and half
the fruit mixture, overlapping
panettone slightly, in cups.
Dollop spoonfuls of remaining
fruit mixture over panettone.
Pour custard over panettone.
5 Place cups in large baking
dish; add enough boiling water
to come halfway up sides of dish.
6 Bake puddings for about
35 minutes or until set. Remove
puddings from baking dish;
stand 10 minutes before serving.
custard Bring cream, milk,
sugar and extract to the boil
in small saucepan. Whisk eggs
in medium bowl; gradually
whisk hot milk mixture into
egg mixture.

makes 6

rosy semi-freddo bombes

3 eggs
3 egg yolks
⅓ cup (75g) caster sugar
⅔ cup (220g) redcurrant jelly
2 tablespoons rosewater
2 cups (500ml) thickened cream
360g white eating chocolate,
    chopped coarsely
2 teaspoons vegetable oil
pink food colouring

1 Whisk eggs, egg yolks and sugar in medium bowl over medium saucepan of simmering water until thick and creamy. Remove from heat; place bowl in larger bowl (or sink) of cold water. Whisk until cold.
2 Meanwhile, melt redcurrant jelly in small saucepan over low heat, stir in rosewater; cool. Whip cream in small bowl with electric mixer until soft peaks form.
3 Stir half the redcurrant mixture into egg mixture; fold in cream. Transfer mixture to large ceramic bowl; cover, freeze overnight.
4 Using a large ice-cream scoop, scoop semi-freddo into balls; place on baking-paper-lined tray. Freeze 2 hours.
5 Cut 12 x 16cm rounds from plastic resealable bags.

6 Stir chocolate and oil in small saucepan over low heat until smooth. Pour half the chocolate mixture into small bowl; tint with colouring. Spread white chocolate over plastic rounds (see page 110); drizzle teaspoons of pink chocolate randomly over each unset chocolate round (see page 111). Gently swirl chocolates together for a marbled effect (see page 111).
7 Drape plastic, chocolate-side down, over balls to enclose; smoothing with hands to avoid deep pleats in the plastic (see page 111). Freeze until firm.
8 Meanwhile, remelt remaining redcurrant mixture in same pan.
9 Peel plastic away from balls (see page 111); stand 5 minutes at room temperature before serving with redcurrant sauce.

makes 12

⅔ cup (160ml) milk
½ cup (125ml) cream
½ vanilla bean
2 egg yolks
¼ cup (55g) caster sugar
1 tablespoon cornflour
25g butter
2 tablespoons bourbon whiskey
450g fresh raspberries
½ cup (160g) raspberry jam,
   warmed, sieved
pastry
1¼ cups (185g) plain flour
¼ cup (55g) caster sugar
125g cold butter, chopped
   coarsely
1 egg yolk

1 Make pastry.
2 Divide pastry into eight portions. Roll portions, one at a time, between sheets of baking paper into rectangles large enough to line eight 5cm x 10cm loose-based flan tins. Lift pastry into tins; press into sides, trim edges. Prick bases all over with fork. Refrigerate 30 minutes. (See page 113.)
3 Preheat oven to 200°C/180°C fan-forced. Place tins on oven tray; line each with baking paper then fill with dried beans or rice (see page 113). Bake 10 minutes. Remove paper and beans from tins; bake further 5 minutes. Cool 15 minutes.
4 Meanwhile, combine milk and cream in small saucepan. Split vanilla bean in half; scrape seeds into pan. Bring to the boil.

5 Beat egg yolks, sugar and cornflour in small bowl with electric mixer until thick and creamy. Gradually beat hot milk mixture into egg mixture. Return mixture to pan; cook, stirring, until mixture boils and thickens. Stir in butter and whiskey; pour warm custard into pastry cases. Refrigerate 3 hours.
6 Top tartlets with raspberries; brush berries with jam.
pastry Process flour, sugar and butter until crumbly. Add egg yolk; process until combined. Knead on floured surface until smooth. Cover; refrigerate 30 minutes.

makes 8

raspberry eggnog tartlets

apple cherry pies

3 medium apples (450g), peeled, chopped finely
¼ cup (55g) caster sugar
1 star anise
2 tablespoons water
300g frozen seeded cherries, quartered
1 tablespoon cornflour
1 egg white
2 teaspoons caster sugar, extra
pastry
1⅔ cups (250g) plain flour
⅓ cup (75g) caster sugar
150g cold butter, chopped coarsely
1 egg yolk

1 Make pastry.
2 Combine apple, sugar, star anise and half of the water in medium saucepan; bring to the boil. Reduce heat; simmer, covered, about 5 minutes or until apple is tender. Add cherries; simmer 2 minutes. Stir in blended cornflour and remaining water; stir over heat until mixture boils and thickens. Remove from heat; cool 10 minutes. Discard star anise.
3 Preheat oven to 200°C/180°C fan-forced.
4 Grease 18 shallow flat-based (2-tablespoon/40ml) patty pan holes. Roll two-thirds of the pastry between sheets of baking paper to 4mm thickness; cut 18 x 6.5cm rounds from pastry. Press rounds into pan holes. Refrigerate 20 minutes.

5 Roll remaining pastry between sheets of baking paper to make a 20cm square; cut into 5mm wide strips. Spoon fruit mixture into pastry cases; brush edge of cases with egg white. Lattice pastry strips over fruit filling. Brush lattice with egg white; sprinkle with extra sugar. Bake about 20 minutes.
6 Stand pies in pan 10 minutes before gently turning out.
pastry Process flour, sugar and butter until crumbly. Add egg yolk; process until combined. Knead on floured surface until smooth. Cover; refrigerate 30 minutes.

makes 18

½ cup (110g) firmly packed
  brown sugar
1 tablespoon cornflour
2 tablespoons maple syrup
25g butter, melted
2 eggs
2 tablespoons cream
1 teaspoon finely grated
  orange rind
1 cup (140g) unsalted
  macadamias
2 teaspoons of icing sugar
pastry
1¼ cups (185g) plain flour
¼ cup (55g) caster sugar
125g cold butter, chopped
  coarsely
1 egg

1 Make pastry.
2 Divide pastry into six portions.
Roll portions, one at a time,
between sheets of baking paper
into rounds large enough to
line six deep 10cm-round loose-
based flan tins. Lift rounds into
tins; press into sides, trim edges.
Prick bases all over with fork.
Refrigerate 30 minutes.
3 Preheat oven to 200°C/180°C
fan-forced. Place tins on oven
tray; line each with baking paper
then fill with dried beans or
uncooked rice. Bake 10 minutes.
Remove paper and beans
carefully from tins; bake a further
5 minutes. Cool pastry cases.

4 Reduce oven temperature to
160°C/140°C fan-forced.
5 Combine brown sugar and
flour in medium bowl; whisk in
syrup, butter, eggs, cream and
rind. Divide nuts among pastry
cases; pour over maple mixture.
Bake about 25 minutes; cool.
Refrigerate tarts for 30 minutes.
6 Serve tarts dusted with sifted
icing sugar.
pastry Process flour, sugar and
butter until crumbly. Add egg;
process until combined. Knead
on floured surface until smooth.
Cover; refrigerate 30 minutes.

makes 6

macadamia & maple tarts

orange blossom delight

You will need to watch the sugar syrup carefully while it simmers for 5 minutes. It may be necessary to lift the pan from the heat several times to help maintain the correct temperature. For perfect results, use an accurate candy thermometer.

¼ cup (45g) powdered gelatine
¼ cup (60ml) hot water
3 cups (660g) caster sugar
2 cups (500ml) cold water
¾ cup (105g) wheaten cornflour
2 tablespoons glucose syrup
1½ tablespoons orange
   flower water
orange food colouring
1 cup (160g) icing sugar

1 Grease deep 19cm-square cake pan.
2 Sprinkle gelatine over the hot water in small bowl.
3 Stir caster sugar and ¾ cup of the cold water in medium saucepan over heat until sugar dissolves; bring to the boil. Boil, without stirring, about 8 minutes or until mixture reaches 116°C on candy thermometer; simmer at this temperature 5 minutes.
4 Meanwhile, blend cornflour in medium saucepan with remaining cold water. Cook, stirring, until mixture boils and thickens. Stir hot sugar syrup, gelatine mixture and glucose into cornflour mixture. Bring to the boil, stirring; reduce heat, simmer, stirring, 10 minutes.
5 Remove mixture from heat; stir in orange flower water and colouring. Strain mixture into pan; skim surface. Stand 15 minutes; cover surface with greased baking paper. Stand overnight at room temperature.
6 Cut orange blossom delight into squares; toss in sifted icing sugar.

makes 36

white chocolate nougat

Use an accurate candy thermometer for perfect results.

1¼ cups (275g) caster sugar
2 tablespoons glucose syrup
2 tablespoons honey
2 tablespoons water
1 egg white
⅔ cup (90g) unsalted pistachios
½ cup (75g) dried blueberries
180g white eating chocolate, chopped coarsely
2 sheets (15cm x 23cm) edible rice paper

1 Stir sugar, glucose, honey and the water in small saucepan over heat, without boiling, until sugar dissolves. Bring to the boil; boil, uncovered, without stirring, about 10 minutes or until syrup reaches 164°C on candy thermometer; remove pan from heat immediately.
2 Beat egg white in small heatproof bowl with electric mixer until soft peaks form. With motor operating, gradually add hot syrup to egg white in a thin steady stream.
3 Meanwhile, have rice paper ready. Working quickly, stir nuts, blueberries and chocolate into nougat. Quickly spoon mixture along long side of each sheet of paper. Roll each sheet to enclose filling and make into a log shape. Wrap each log in foil; roll on bench to make perfect log shape.
4 Stand about 2 hours or until cool. Serve cut into slices.

makes 40

truffle trio

dark chocolate truffles
200g dark eating chocolate,
  chopped finely
2 tablespoons cream
2 tablespoons muscat
3 sheets gold leaf
orange & ginger truffles
200g dark eating chocolate,
  chopped finely
¼ cup (60ml) cream
2 tablespoons Grand Marnier
⅓ cup (75g) finely chopped
  glacé ginger
¼ cup (25g) cocoa powder
chocolate chilli truffles
200g dark eating chocolate,
  chopped finely
⅓ cup (60ml) cream
1 fresh long red chilli, seeded,
  chopped finely
300g dark eating chocolate,
  melted

dark chocolate truffles
1 Stir chocolate, cream and
muscat in small saucepan over
low heat until smooth. Transfer
mixture to small bowl; refrigerate
3 hours.
2 Working with a quarter of
the chocolate mixture at a time
(keep remaining mixture in
the refrigerator), roll rounded
teaspoons of mixture into balls;
place on tray. Refrigerate truffles
until firm.
3 Using tweezers or a fine paint
brush, decorate truffles with
small pieces of gold leaf (see
page 115).
orange & ginger truffles
1 Stir chocolate, cream and
liqueur in small saucepan over
low heat until smooth; stir in
ginger. Transfer mixture to small
bowl; refrigerate 3 hours.
2 Working with a quarter of
the chocolate mixture at a time
(keep remaining mixture in
the refrigerator), roll rounded
teaspoons of mixture into balls;
place on tray. Refrigerate truffles
until firm.
3 Roll truffles in sifted cocoa
before serving.

chocolate chilli truffles
1 Stir chopped chocolate and
cream in small saucepan over
low heat until smooth; stir in
chilli. Transfer mixture to small
bowl; refrigerate 3 hours.
2 Working with a quarter of
the chocolate mixture at a time
(keep remaining mixture in
the refrigerator), roll rounded
teaspoons of mixture into balls;
place on tray. Refrigerate truffles
until firm.
3 Working quickly, dip truffles
into melted chocolate, roll gently
with hands to coat evenly; return
to tray. Refrigerate until firm.

makes 20 of each truffle

If you have trouble stacking the truffles, secure them through the centre of the truffles with strong wooden toothpicks.

360g white eating chocolate, chopped coarsely
⅓ cup (80ml) cream
2 tablespoons Malibu
1 cup (80g) desiccated coconut
3 unsalted pistachios, halved
9 dried cranberries

1 Stir chocolate, cream and liqueur in small saucepan over low heat until smooth. Transfer mixture to small bowl; refrigerate 3 hours.
2 Roll two level teaspoons of mixture into balls to make six small balls, roll three level teaspoons of mixture into balls to make six medium balls, roll level tablespoons of mixture into balls to make six large balls (you will have 18 truffles); place on tray. Refrigerate until truffles are firm.
3 Roll truffles in coconut; assemble six snowmen using three of the different-sized truffles for each. Decorate snowmen with pieces of trimmed pistachio halves for noses and small pieces of cranberries for eyes. Use scraps of fabric, tinsel or ribbon to make scarves.

makes 6

coconut truffle snowmen

fruit butters

Make sure you grate the rind from the citrus fruit before juicing. Keep the butters in the refrigerator. These gift-friendly butters make wonderful spreads for toast, muffins or pikelets.

passionfruit butter
4 eggs, beaten lightly, strained
185g unsalted butter,
   chopped coarsely
¾ cup (165g) caster sugar
⅓ cup (80ml) lemon juice
1 cup (250ml) passionfruit pulp
lime butter
4 eggs, beaten lightly, strained
185g unsalted butter,
   chopped coarsely
1½ cups (225g) caster sugar
½ cup (125ml) lime juice
¼ cup (60ml) lemon juice
1 tablespoon finely grated
   lime rind
green food colouring
blood orange butter
4 eggs, beaten lightly, strained
185g unsalted butter,
   chopped coarsely
¾ cup (165g) caster sugar
1 cup (250ml) blood orange juice
1 tablespoon finely grated
   blood orange rind

1 For the passionfruit butter, combine ingredients in medium heatproof bowl over medium saucepan of simmering water. Stir until mixture thickly coats the back of a wooden spoon. Remove from heat immediately.
2 Stand bowl in sink of cold water, stirring occasionally, for about 10 minutes to stop cooking process. Pour into hot sterilised jars; seal.
3 For lime butter, combine ingredients except rind and colouring in medium heatproof bowl; cook as per passionfruit butter. Stir in rind and colouring before pouring into jars.
4 For blood orange butter, combine ingredients except rind in medium heatproof bowl; cook as per passionfruit butter. Stir in rind before pouring into jars.

makes 3 cups of each butter

trio of jams

brandied cherry jam
900g frozen seeded cherries
¾ cup (180ml) water
¼ cup (60ml) lemon juice
½ cup (125ml) cherry brandy
4 cups (880g) white sugar,
approximately

1 Combine cherries, the water and juice in large saucepan; bring to the boil. Reduce heat; simmer, covered, about 10 minutes or until cherries are soft. Stir in brandy.
2 Measure fruit mixture; allow ¾ cup (165g) sugar for each cup of mixture. Return mixture and sugar to pan; stir over heat, without boiling, until sugar dissolves. Boil, uncovered, about 40 minutes or until jam sets when tested on a cold saucer (see page 113).
3 Pour into hot sterilised jars; seal immediately.

makes 1 litre (4 cups)

spiced fig & apple jam
Finely grate the rind from the oranges before juicing them.

2 large granny smith apples
(500g), peeled, chopped finely
2 cups (500ml) water
16 medium fresh figs (1 kg),
chopped coarsely
½ cup (125ml) orange juice
1.1kg (5 cups) caster sugar,
approximately
2 tablespoons finely grated
orange rind
3 star anise
1 cinnamon stick, halved
2 vanilla beans, halved
lengthways

1 Combine apple and the water in large saucepan; bring to the boil. Reduce heat; simmer, covered, about 20 minutes or until apples are soft. Add figs and juice; simmer, covered, 10 minutes.
2 Measure fruit mixture; allow ¾ cup (165g) sugar for each cup of mixture. Return mixture and sugar to pan with remaining ingredients; stir over heat, without boiling, until sugar dissolves. Boil, uncovered, about 45 minutes or until jam sets when tested on a cold saucer (see page 113).
3 Pour into hot sterilised jars; seal immediately.

makes 2 litres (8 cups)

citrus marmalade
Lime rind will take the longest time to cook, so it's the one to check; it must be very soft.

4 large oranges (1.2kg)
3 medium lemons (420g)
4 large limes (400g)
1.25 litres (5 cups) water
1.6kg (7 cups) white sugar,
approximately

1 Peel all fruit thinly; cut rind into thin strips. Remove pith from all fruit; reserve half, discard remaining pith. Chop flesh coarsely, reserve seeds.
2 Combine flesh and rind in large bowl with the water. Tie reserved pith and seeds in muslin (see page 113); add to bowl. Stand at room temperature overnight.
3 Place fruit mixture and bag in large saucepan; bring to the boil. Simmer, covered, 25 minutes or until rind is soft. Discard bag.
4 Measure fruit mixture; allow 1 cup (220g) sugar for each cup of mixture. Return mixture and sugar to pan; stir over heat, without boiling, until sugar dissolves. Boil, uncovered, about 40 minutes or until marmalade sets when tested on a cold saucer (see page 113).
5 Pour into hot sterilised jars; seal immediately.

makes 1.75 litres (7 cups)

peach cardamom chutney

Chutney will keep for at least 6 months if the jars have been sterilised correctly. Store the jars in a cool dark place – the refrigerator is best.

7 large peaches (1.5kg)
1 large brown onion (200g), chopped finely
¾ cup (120g) coarsely chopped raisins
1½ cups (330g) firmly packed brown sugar
¾ cup (180ml) cider vinegar
1 cinnamon stick
4 cardamom pods, bruised
1 teaspoon whole allspice
2 teaspoons finely grated lemon rind

1 Cut small cross in bottom of each peach. Lower peaches gently into large saucepan of boiling water, boil for 1 minute, then place in large bowl of cold water. Peel peaches, remove stones, chop peaches coarsely.
2 Combine peaches with remaining ingredients in large saucepan; stir over heat until sugar dissolves. Bring to the boil; reduce heat. Simmer, uncovered, stirring occasionally, about 45 minutes or until thick.
3 Pour chutney into hot sterilised jars; seal immediately.

makes 2 litres (8 cups)

Store this relish in the refrigerator for up to 3 months. Once opened, it will keep for several weeks in the refrigerator.

50g butter
3 large red onions (900g),
    sliced thinly
1kg frozen cranberries
2 cups (440g) firmly packed
    brown sugar
1 cup (250ml) brown vinegar
½ cup (125ml) balsamic vinegar
1 teaspoon coarse cooking salt
4 whole cloves
½ teaspoon dried chilli flakes

1 Melt butter in large saucepan; cook onion, stirring, until soft.
2 Add remaining ingredients; stir over heat until sugar dissolves. Bring to the boil; reduce heat. Simmer, uncovered, stirring occasionally, for about 1 hour or until thick.
3 Pour relish into hot sterilised jars; seal immediately.

makes 1.5 litres (6 cups)

cranberry & red onion relish

chilli jam

Chilli jam is really hot and you will find a little goes a long way. If you want to decrease the heat dramatically, remove the seeds from the chillies – use disposable gloves to do this. The jam is best poured into small jars, it will keep indefinitely if the jars have been sterilised correctly. Store the jam in a cool dark place. Once opened, store in the refrigerator.

750g fresh long red chillies, chopped coarsely
vegetable oil, for deep-frying
3 large brown onions (600g), chopped coarsely
16 shallots (400g), chopped coarsely
10 cloves garlic, peeled, chopped coarsely
10cm piece fresh ginger (50g), peeled, chopped coarsely
1 cup (200g) coarsely chopped palm sugar
¼ cup (85g) tamarind pulp
⅓ cup (80ml) fish sauce

1 Deep-fry chillies, in batches, in hot oil until soft. Drain on absorbent paper. Reheat oil; deep-fry combined onions, shallots, garlic and ginger, in batches, until browned lightly. Drain on absorbent paper.
2 Combine vegetables with 1 cup (250ml) of the cooking oil in large bowl. Process, in batches, until almost smooth.
3 Cook chilli mixture in large heavy-based saucepan over low heat, stirring, for about 10 minutes. Add sugar; cook, stirring, 10 minutes. Add remaining ingredients; cook over low heat, stirring occasionally, about 2 hours or until thick and dark red in colour.
4 Pour jam into hot sterilised jars; seal immediately.

makes 1.5 litres (6 cups)

1 tablespoon instant coffee
 granules
1 tablespoon boiling water
1½ tablespoons chocolate-
 flavoured topping
350ml Irish whiskey
1¾ cups (460ml) cream
395g can condensed milk
1 egg
1 teaspoon coconut essence

1 Dissolve coffee in the water in a large jug; stir in topping.
2 Whisk in remaining ingredients. Strain mixture into cooled sterilised bottles; seal immediately.
3 Store liqueur in refrigerator for up to 6 months.

makes 1.25 litres (5 cups)

irish crème liqueur

pomegranate punch

You will need about eight large pomegranates (3kg) for the syrup. You can use sparkling water instead of champagne for a non-alcoholic punch. Leftover pomegranate syrup can be used as a cordial. Mix about 1 part of the syrup to about 4 parts of still or sparkling water.

120g fresh raspberries
750ml bottle chilled champagne
1 litre (4 cups) chilled
    unsweetened cranberry juice
1 cup firmly packed mint leaves
pomegranate syrup
1 kg (4½ cups) caster sugar
2 cups (500ml) water
2 cups pomegranate pulp
    (see page 114)
2 tablespoons lemon juice

1 Place about three raspberries in each hole of a 16-hole (1-tablespoon/20ml) ice cube tray. Pour water over raspberries to fill holes. Freeze about 3 hours or until set.
2 Make pomegranate syrup.
3 Place 1 cup (250ml) of the pomegranate syrup in a large serving bowl (reserve remaining syrup for another use). Stir in champagne and cranberry juice. Add mint and raspberry ice cubes; serve immediately.
pomegranate syrup Stir sugar and the water in medium saucepan over heat until sugar dissolves. Bring to the boil; simmer, without stirring, about 10 minutes or until thickened slightly. Add pomegranate pulp and juice; bring to the boil. Reduce heat, simmer 2 minutes. Remove pan from heat; stand 10 minutes. Strain into hot sterilised bottle; seal immediately. Store in refrigerator for up to 3 months.

serves 8

fruit mince tarts

You need to reserve 100g of pastry scraps – if you don't have scales, 100g of scraps (pushed together) would be about the same size as a small apple.

1½ cups (430g) cranberry & apple fruit mince (see page 78)
pastry
1⅔ cups (250g) plain flour
⅓ cup (75g) caster sugar
150g cold butter, chopped coarsely
1 egg yolk
streusel topping
½ teaspoon ground cinnamon
¼ teaspoon mixed spice
100g pastry scraps
marzipan topping
100g marzipan
2 tablespoons icing sugar
1 egg yolk
meringue topping
1 egg white
¼ cup (55g) caster sugar

1 Make pastry.
2 Grease 18 deep flat-based (2-tablespoon/40ml) patty pan holes. Roll dough between sheets of baking paper to 3mm thickness; cut 18 x 6.5cm rounds from dough. Press rounds into pan holes; prick bases well with fork. Refrigerate 30 minutes.
3 Preheat oven to 200°C/180°C fan-forced. Bake pastry cases 5 minutes; cool.
4 Make streusel topping by kneading spices into pastry scraps; cover, freeze 1 hour or until firm.
5 Meanwhile, make marzipan topping by kneading marzipan in a little of the sifted icing sugar until pliable. Dust bench with a little more of the sifted icing sugar; roll out marzipan to 3mm thickness. Cut six 5.5cm rounds from marzipan. Cut a 3.5cm snowflake from centre of each round. Remove and discard cut-out snowflake.

6 Spoon fruit mince into pastry cases. Grate streusel topping over six of the tarts. Place marzipan rounds on another six tarts; brush with egg yolk, dust with remaining sifted icing sugar. Bake these 12 tarts about 8 minutes or until browned lightly.
7 Increase oven to 220°C/200°C fan-forced.
8 Meanwhile, make meringue topping by beating egg white in small bowl with electric mixer until soft peaks form. Gradually add sugar; beating until sugar dissolves.
9 Pipe meringue onto remaining six tarts; bake about 5 minutes or until browned.
pastry Blend or process flour, sugar and butter until crumbly. Add egg yolk; process until combined. Knead pastry on floured surface until smooth. Cover; refrigerate 30 minutes.

makes 18

You will need to buy a total of 6 slices of glacé orange for this recipe.

⅔ cup (100g) plain flour
1 cup (190g) coarsely chopped dried figs
1 cup (140g) coarsely chopped seeded dried dates
2 slices (45g) finely chopped glacé orange
1 cup (160g) blanched almonds, roasted
1 cup (140g) roasted hazelnuts
1 cup (140g) roasted macadamias
⅓ cup (115g) honey
⅔ cup (150g) firmly packed brown sugar
2 tablespoons Grand Marnier
100g dark eating chocolate, melted
4 slices glacé orange (90g)

1 Preheat oven to 150°C/130°C fan-forced. Grease four deep 10cm-round cake pans; line bases with baking paper.
2 Sift flour into large bowl; stir in figs, dates, chopped glacé orange and nuts.
3 Stir honey, sugar and liqueur in small saucepan over heat, without boiling, until sugar dissolves. Simmer, uncovered, without stirring, 5 minutes. Pour hot syrup, then chocolate into nut mixture; mix well.
4 Press mixture firmly into pans; top each with a slice of glacé orange.
5 Bake panforte about 25 minutes; cool in pans. Remove panforte from pans; wrap in foil. Stand overnight.

makes 4

jaffa panforte

cranberry & apple fruit mince

Fruit mince makes a beautiful gift. It will keep in the refrigerator for at least 12 months. If you can't find dried cherries, use the equivalent amount of extra dried cranberries instead.

2⅔ cups (325g) dried cranberries
2½ cups (200g) finely chopped dried apples
2 cups (320g) finely chopped raisins
1 cup (250g) finely chopped dried cherries
¾ cup (150g) finely chopped dried figs
½ cup (85g) mixed peel
½ cup (115g) glacé ginger, chopped finely
3 medium apples (450g), peeled, grated coarsely
1½ cups (330g) firmly packed brown sugar
½ cup (160g) raspberry jam
1 tablespoon finely grated orange rind
¼ cup (60ml) orange juice
2 teaspoons mixed spice
½ teaspoon ground clove
1 cinnamon stick, halved
1⅓ cups (330ml) Grand Marnier

1 Mix ingredients in large bowl until combined.
2 Cover bowl with plastic wrap. Store mixture in a cool dry place for a month before using; stir mixture every two or three days.

makes 9½ cups (2.5kg)

Candied clementines are available from specialty food stores and delicatessens.

150g dark eating chocolate
1 cup (170g) coarsely chopped dried figs
¾ cup (100g) dried cherries
1 teaspoon finely grated orange rind
¼ cup (60ml) brandy
⅔ cup (90g) unsalted coarsely chopped roasted pistachios
⅔ cup (70g) coarsely chopped roasted walnuts
⅓ cup (60g) finely chopped candied clementines
¼ cup (55g) finely chopped glacé ginger
½ teaspoon ground cinnamon
¼ teaspoon mixed spice
2 sheets (15cm x 23cm) edible rice paper

1 Chop half of the chocolate finely. Chop remaining chocolate coarsely, melt in small heatproof bowl over small saucepan of simmering water.
2 Process figs, cherries, rind and half of the brandy until fruit is chopped finely. Transfer mixture to large bowl; stir in nuts, clementines, ginger, spices, chopped and melted chocolate.
3 Spoon mixture along long side of each rice paper sheet. Roll each sheet to enclose filling and make a log shape. Pinch along top of each log to make a triangle shape; brush rice paper with remaining brandy.
4 Wrap fruit and nut logs in baking paper; stand overnight at room temperature. Serve logs sliced thickly.

makes 2

fruit & nut logs

duet of grapefruit jellies

If the ruby grapefruit juice isn't bright enough, add a little red food colouring to the gelatine mixture.

1 cup (220g) white sugar
ruby jellies
1 tablespoon powdered gelatine
1 cup (250ml) finely strained ruby grapefruit juice
½ cup (110g) white sugar
2 tablespoons glucose syrup
golden jellies
1 tablespoon powdered gelatine
1 cup (250ml) finely strained grapefruit juice
½ cup (110g) white sugar
2 tablespoons glucose syrup
yellow food colouring

1 Make ruby jellies by sprinkling gelatine over half of the juice in small heatproof jug, stand jug in small saucepan of simmering water. Stir until gelatine dissolves.
2 Stir sugar, syrup and remaining juice in small saucepan over low heat until sugar dissolves. Remove from heat, stir in gelatine mixture. Pour mixture into deep 15cm-square cake pan; refrigerate overnight or until set.
3 Make golden jellies following ruby jellies method; add the food colouring with the gelatine mixture.
4 Cut jellies into squares using hot dry knife in pan; toss in extra sugar just before serving.

makes 25 of each flavour

triple chocolate fudge

For success every time, you will need to use an accurate candy thermometer for this recipe.

1½ cups (330g) caster sugar
½ cup (110g) firmly packed brown sugar
100g dark eating chocolate, chopped coarsely
2 tablespoons glucose syrup
½ cup (125ml) cream
¼ cup (60ml) milk
40g butter
200g white eating chocolate, melted
50g milk eating chocolate, melted

1 Grease and line an 8cm x 26cm bar cake pan with baking paper, extending paper 2cm above the sides of the pan.
2 Stir sugars, dark chocolate, syrup, cream and milk in small saucepan over heat, without boiling, until sugars dissolve. Bring to the boil; boil without stirring, about 10 minutes or until mixture reaches 116°C on candy thermometer. (See page 114.) Remove pan immediately from heat, leaving thermometer in mixture; add butter, do not stir.
3 Cool fudge about 40 minutes or until mixture drops to 40°C. Remove thermometer. Stir fudge with wooden spoon about 10 minutes or until a small amount dropped from spoon holds its shape (see page 114). Spread fudge into cake pan; smooth surface. Cover with foil; stand at room temperature 2 hours.

4 Spread white chocolate over fudge, drizzle with milk chocolate. Pull a skewer through the chocolate topping for a marbled affect. Refrigerate fudge for 3 hours or overnight.
5 Remove fudge from pan, cut in half lengthways before slicing thinly.

makes 50

runny chocolate fruit puddings

½ cup (160g) bottled fruit mince
50g dark eating chocolate
   (70% cocoa solids),
   chopped coarsely
150g butter, chopped coarsely
3 eggs
⅓ cup (75g) firmly packed
   brown sugar
½ cup (75g) plain flour
¼ cup (35g) self-raising flour
1 tablespoon cocoa powder
chocolate rum sauce
150g dark eating chocolate
   (70% cocoa solids),
   chopped coarsely
⅓ cup (80ml) cream
2 tablespoons dark rum

1 Spoon fruit mince into 6 holes of a 1 tablespoon (20ml) ice cube tray; freeze for 3 hours.
2 Preheat oven to 200°C/180°C fan-forced. Grease six 1-cup (250ml) pudding moulds.
3 Stir chocolate and butter in small saucepan over low heat until smooth. Cool 10 minutes.
4 Beat eggs and sugar in small bowl with electric mixer until thick and creamy; transfer mixture to medium bowl. Fold in sifted flours and cocoa, then chocolate mixture.
5 Spoon chocolate mixture into moulds. Remove frozen fruit mince cubes from tray; press one cube into centre of each pudding.
6 Bake puddings 12 minutes.
7 Meanwhile, make chocolate rum sauce. Serve puddings drizzled with sauce.
chocolate rum sauce Stir ingredients in small saucepan over low heat until smooth.

serves 6

mini gingerbread houses

3 cups (450g) self-raising flour
¾ cup (165g) firmly packed
   brown sugar
1 tablespoon ground ginger
1 teaspoon ground cinnamon
1 teaspoon ground nutmeg
½ teaspoon ground clove
185g butter, softened
¾ cup (270g) golden syrup
1 egg
1 cup (70g) All-bran
silver cachous
assorted lollies
2 tablespoons pure icing sugar
royal icing
3 cups (480g) pure icing sugar,
   approximately
2 egg whites

1 Process flour, sugar, spices and butter until mixture is crumbly. Add syrup and egg; process until combined. Knead dough on floured surface until smooth. Cover; refrigerate 1 hour.
2 Meanwhile, cut out paper patterns for gingerbread houses. Cut two 7cm x 9cm rectangles for roof; two 6cm squares for side walls, and two 7cm x 9cm rectangles for front and back walls. Trim front and back walls to form two 6cm high gables.
3 Preheat oven to 180°C/160°C fan-forced. Roll dough between sheets of baking paper to 5mm thickness. Peel away top paper; use patterns to cut shapes from dough. Pull away excess dough around shapes; slide baking paper with shapes onto oven trays, bake about 12 minutes or until shapes are slightly firm.
4 While shapes are still warm and soft, use tip of sharp knife to trim all shapes to straighten sides; transfer shapes to wire rack to cool.

5 Make royal icing.
6 Assemble houses, securing rooves and walls together with icing. If possible, stand houses several hours or overnight, supporting sides with four cans, so that they are thoroughly dry before decorating. Spread royal icing onto rooves, decorate with bran and cachous. Decorate houses with lollies, securing with royal icing. Dust house with a little sifted icing sugar.
royal icing Sift icing sugar through very fine sieve. Lightly beat egg whites in small bowl with electric mixer; beat in icing sugar, a tablespoon at a time. Continue beating until icing reaches firm peaks; cover tightly with plastic wrap until ready to use.

makes 4

wicked dark chocolate ice-cream

Candied clementines are available from specialty food stores and delicatessens.

1¾ cups (430ml) milk
600ml cream
1 tablespoon cocoa powder
400g dark eating chocolate, chopped coarsely
8 egg yolks
¾ cup (165g) caster sugar
2 tablespoons Cointreau
6 whole candied clementines
2 teaspoons vegetable oil
2 teaspoons cocoa powder

1 Combine milk, cream, sifted cocoa and 100g of the chocolate in medium saucepan; bring to the boil, stirring.

2 Meanwhile, whisk egg yolks and sugar in medium bowl until thick and creamy; gradually whisk into hot milk mixture. Stir custard over low heat, without boiling, until thickened slightly. Stir in liqueur. Cover surface of custard with plastic wrap; cool 20 minutes.

3 Strain custard into shallow container, such as aluminium slab cake pan, cover with foil; freeze until almost firm.

4 Place ice-cream in large bowl, chop coarsely, beat with electric mixer until smooth. Pour into deep container, cover; freeze until firm. Repeat process two more times.

5 Line six 1-cup (250ml) moulds with plastic wrap. Stand ice-cream at room temperature to soften slightly; spoon half of the softened ice-cream into the moulds. Using the back of a teaspoon, make a shallow hollow in the centre of ice-cream. Place one clementine in each hollow; top with remaining ice-cream. Smooth surface; cover, freeze 3 hours or until firm. Turn puddings onto a tray; return to freezer.

6 Cut six 14cm rounds from plastic wrap or resealable bags. Stir remaining chocolate and oil in small saucepan over low heat until smooth. Spread melted chocolate over plastic wrap then quickly drape plastic, chocolate-side down, over puddings. Quickly smooth with hands, to avoid making deep pleats in the plastic. Freeze until firm; peel away plastic.

7 Serve ice-cream dusted with sifted cocoa.

makes 6

orange pudding with rum sauce

1 large orange (300g)
10g butter, melted
2 tablespoons brown sugar
90g butter, softened
¾ cup (165g) caster sugar
2 teaspoons finely grated
   orange rind
2 eggs
1¼ cups (185g) self-raising flour
⅓ cup (50g) plain flour
½ cup (125ml) milk
rum sauce
50g butter
⅓ cup (115g) golden syrup
¼ cup (55g) firmly packed
   brown sugar
2 tablespoons dark rum

1 Slice unpeeled orange thinly using a mandolin, V-slicer or sharp knife to 4mm thickness.
2 Brush 2-litre (8-cup) pudding steamer evenly with the melted butter. Sift brown sugar into steamer; shake to coat sides of steamer evenly with sugar. Arrange orange slices over bottom and around the side of the steamer so that the slices around the side touch the orange on the bottom of the steamer.
3 Beat softened butter, caster sugar and rind in small bowl with electric mixer until light and fluffy; beat in eggs one at a time. Transfer mixture to medium bowl; stir in sifted flours and milk in two batches.
4 Spread mixture into steamer. Cover with pleated baking paper and foil; secure with lid.

5 Place pudding steamer in large saucepan with enough boiling water to come halfway up side of steamer; cover pan with tight lid. Boil 1 hour, replenishing water as necessary to maintain level. Stand pudding 5 minutes before turning out.
6 Meanwhile, make rum sauce.
7 Serve pudding with sauce.
rum sauce Stir butter, syrup and sugar in small saucepan over low heat until sugar dissolves; bring to the boil. Reduce heat; simmer, uncovered, 3 minutes or until thickened slightly. Remove from heat; stir in rum.

serves 8

You can buy brandied cumquats from specialty food stores and delicatessens. Or, to make your own, see page 101.

2 cups (500g) drained brandied
  cumquats
185g butter, softened
1 cup (220g) caster sugar
3 eggs
1 cup (150g) self-raising flour
¾ cup (90g) almond meal
2 teaspoons icing sugar
marmalade syrup
½ cup (110g) caster sugar
¾ cup (180ml) water
⅓ cup (115g) orange marmalade
2 tablespoons brandied
  cumquat liquid

1 Preheat oven to 180°C/160°C fan-forced. Grease eight 1-cup (250ml) ovenproof dishes or tea cups. Place on oven trays.
2 Reserve one cumquat for later use; blend drained remaining cumquats until pulpy (you will need 1 cup pulp).
3 Beat butter and sugar in small bowl with electric mixer until light and fluffy; beat in eggs one at a time. Transfer mixture to medium bowl; stir in sifted flour, almond meal and cumquat pulp.
4 Spoon mixture into dishes; bake, uncovered, 40 minutes
5 Meanwhile, make marmalade syrup.
6 Pour half of the hot syrup over the hot puddings; dust with sifted icing sugar. Serve topped with segments cut from reserved cumquat and remaining syrup.

marmalade syrup Stir sugar and the water in small saucepan over low heat, without boiling, until sugar dissolves. Bring to the boil; add marmalade. Reduce heat, simmer, uncovered, about 5 minutes or until syrup is slightly thickened. Stir in reserved brandy syrup.

makes 8

brandied cumquat puddings

white christmas ice-cream

1 vanilla bean
1¾ cups (430ml) milk
600ml cream
180g white eating chocolate,
    chopped coarsely
8 egg yolks
¾ cup (165g) caster sugar
1 cup (130g) dried cranberries
2 tablespoons brandy
1 cup (140g) unsalted pistachios
2 teaspoons vegetable oil

1 Split vanilla bean lengthways; scrape seeds into medium saucepan. Add pod, milk, cream and 50g of the chocolate; bring to the boil.

2 Meanwhile, whisk egg yolks and sugar in medium bowl until thick and creamy; gradually whisk into hot milk mixture. Stir custard over low heat, without boiling, until thickened slightly. Cover surface of custard with plastic wrap; cool 20 minutes.

3 Strain custard into shallow container, such as aluminium slab cake pan, cover with foil; freeze until almost firm.

4 Place ice-cream in large bowl, chop coarsely; beat with electric mixer until smooth. Pour into deep container, cover; freeze until firm. Repeat process two more times

5 Meanwhile, place cranberries and brandy in small bowl; stand 15 minutes.

6 Stir cranberry mixture and nuts into ice-cream. Spoon ice-cream into eight ¾-cup (180ml) moulds. Cover, freeze 3 hours or until firm.

7 Stir remaining chocolate and oil in small saucepan over low heat until smooth.

8 Dip each mould, one at a time, into a bowl of hot water for about 1 second. Turn ice-creams onto serving plates; top with warm chocolate mixture.

makes 8

mini christmas puddings

This recipe makes six single generous servings; each pudding will weigh about 360g. You need six 30cm squares of unbleached calico for each pudding cloth. If calico has not been used before, soak in cold water overnight; next day, boil it 20 minutes then rinse in cold water. Puddings can be cooked in two boilers or in batches, mixture will keep at room temperature for several hours.

1 cup (170g) raisins, chopped coarsely
1 cup (160g) sultanas
1 cup (150g) finely chopped seeded dried dates
½ cup (95g) finely chopped seeded prunes
½ cup (85g) mixed peel
½ cup (125g) finely chopped glacé apricots
1 teaspoon finely grated lemon rind
2 tablespoons lemon juice
2 tablespoons apricot jam
2 tablespoons brandy
250g butter, softened
2 cups (440g) firmly packed brown sugar
5 eggs
1¼ cups (185g) plain flour
½ teaspoon ground nutmeg
½ teaspoon mixed spice
4 cups (280g) stale breadcrumbs

1 Combine fruit, rind, juice, jam and brandy in large bowl; mix well. Cover tightly with plastic wrap; store in a cool, dark place for one week, stirring every day.
2 Beat butter and sugar in small bowl with electric mixer until combined; beat in eggs one at a time. Add butter mixture to fruit mixture, mix well, then mix in sifted dry ingredients and breadcrumbs.
3 Fill boiler three-quarters full of hot water, cover with a tight lid; bring to the boil. Have ready 1m lengths of kitchen string and an extra 1 cup of plain flour. Wearing thick rubber gloves, dip cloths, one at a time, into boiling water; boil 1 minute then remove, squeeze excess water from cloth. Spread hot cloth on bench, rub 2 tablespoons of the flour into centre of each cloth to cover an area about 18cm in diameter, leaving flour a little thicker in centre of cloth where "skin" on the pudding needs to be thickest (see page 115).
4 Divide pudding mixture among cloths; placing in centre of each cloth. Gather cloths around mixture, avoiding any deep pleats; pat into round shapes. Tie cloths tightly with string as close to mixture as possible (see page 115). Tie loops in string.

5 Lower three puddings into the boiling water; tie ends of string to handles of boiler to suspend puddings (see page 115). Cover, boil 2 hours, replenishing water as necessary.
6 Untie puddings from handles; place wooden spoons through string loops. Do not put puddings on bench; suspend from spoon by placing over rungs of upturned stool or wedging handle in drawer. Twist ends of cloth around string to avoid them touching puddings; hang 10 minutes.
7 Place puddings on board; cut string, carefully peel back cloth. Turn puddings onto a plate then carefully peel cloth away completely; cool. Stand at least 20 minutes or until skin darkens and pudding becomes firm.

makes 6

brandied cumquats

Buy cumquats when they are in season (autumn to spring), brandy them and store them for at least 2 months before Christmas. Drink the flavoured brandy as you would a liqueur or, serve the cumquats with ice-cream and a little of the brandy. Or, use the cumquats in pies, puddings, cakes and crumbles. Make the brandied cumquats in one large or several small jars. Or, decant the mixture into smaller gift-sized jars after the standing time has passed.

750g cumquats
2 cinnamon sticks, halved
  lengthways
2 vanilla beans, halved
  lengthways
3 cups (660g) caster sugar
2½ cups (625ml) brandy

1 Place clean jars (and lids) on their sides in a large saucepan; cover jars completely with cold water. Put the lid on the pan, bring to the boil, boil for 20 minutes. Remove the jars carefully from the water; drain upright (to allow the water to evaporate) on the sink until the jars are dry.
2 Meanwhile, wash and dry the cumquats well, then prick each one several times with a fine skewer or a thick needle.
3 Place the cumquats, cinnamon and vanilla in the jars; pour over enough of the combined sugar and brandy to cover the cumquats completely. Seal.
4 Stand the jars in a cool, dark place for at least 2 months before using. Invert the jars every few days to help dissolve the sugar.

makes 7 cups (1.75 litres)

1½ cups (225g) plain flour
¾ cup (165g) firmly packed
    dark muscovado sugar
2 teaspoons ground ginger
1 teaspoon mixed spice
¼ teaspoon ground clove
150g butter, chopped coarsely
1 egg yolk
¼ cup (55g) raw sugar

1 Process flour, muscovado sugar, spices and butter until crumbly. Add egg yolk; process until combined. Knead dough on floured surface until smooth. Cover; refrigerate 30 minutes.
2 Divide dough in half; roll each half between sheets of baking paper to 3mm thickness. Refrigerate 30 minutes.
3 Preheat oven to 180°C/160°C fan-forced. Line three oven trays with baking paper.
4 Cut thirty 7cm rounds from dough. Place rounds on trays; sprinkle with raw sugar.
5 Bake snaps about 10 minutes; cool on trays.

makes 30

sugar & spice snaps

Window box

Let your gorgeous homemade treats be the star. Carefully cut a rectangle in the lid of a cardboard gift box. Use cello/sticky tape to attach a piece of acetate, available from newsagents, to the underside of the lid to create a window. Line the box with tissue paper and tie all up with a ribbon to match.

Tiny takeaways

Line little paper pails, available from cheap variety or haberdashery stores, with patterned waxed tissue paper. Gently place little Christmas goodies in them such as cookies, brownies or macaroons. Finish off with gift tags personalised with a cute stamp bought from a stationery store, tied on with metallic string.

Festive bottles

For an authentic home-made presentation for the irish crème liqueur or pomegranate punch, use sterilised recycled bottles or bought hinge-lidded bottles, available from supermarkets. Attach your own labels endorsed with a personalised message. Glue together two contrasting pieces of coloured paper, one smaller than the other, to get the effect pictured here.

gift packaging

Turn the gorgeous treats in this book into heartfelt gifts with striking packaging. Start with these ideas then let your imagination run wild.

Sweet satchels
Show off luscious, eat-me treats like stained glass Christmas cookies, or jewelled rocky road in a cellophane bag from variety or haberdashery stores. Fold the top of the bag neatly and slip some folded fabric or coloured paper over the top. Secure by using a hole-punch to cut two holes, then tying yarn or ribbon through the holes.

Decorative jars
For a traditional way to present jams, chutney, relish and fruit mince, use sterilised recycled jam jars decorated with felt and an ornate paper doily. Using pinking shears, cut a circle of felt about 2 cm larger than the doily, then secure to the top of the jar using string, wool or ribbon. Make your own tags or labels.

Beautiful boxes
Tarts, truffles and fragile cookies look beautiful nestled in decorative paper. Dress up the box using a rectangle of coloured paper, fabric or even magazine cuttings wrapped neatly around both base and lid. Fasten to the box with string or wool, wrapping around several times to create the effect you see here and finish with a handmade gift tag.

1. Oven trays

2. Deep round cake pans

3. Deep round loose-based flan tin (8cm base, 10cm top)

4. Rectangular loose-based flan tin (5cm x 10cm)

5. Candy thermometer

6. Round cutters

7. Star-shaped cutters

8. Bell-shaped cutter

9. Christmas cutters
Clockwise from angel cutter, holly leaf, small tree, moon, star, snowflake, large tree

10. Pudding steamer with lid (2-litre/8-cup capacity)

11. Standard patty or muffin pan (⅓-cup/80ml capacity)

12. Wooden skewers

13. Bar cake pan (8cm x 26cm)

14. Mandolin (also known as a V-slicer)

15. Shallow flat-based patty pan (2-tablespoon/40ml capacity)

equipment

10

11

12

13

14

19

22

20

16

17

18

21

23

15

16. Ice-cream scoop
17. Calico
18. Kitchen string
19. Foil paper cases
20. Tweezers
21. Paint brush
22. Resealable strong plastic bags for piping

23. 170g Passionfruit pulp cans (5.5cm diameter, 8.5cm tall)
24. Piping bags
25. Large plastic piping tube
26. Texas muffin pan (¾ cup/ 180ml capacity)
27. Mini paper patty cases
28. Pudding moulds

29. Deep square cake pan
30. Slice pan (19cm x 29cm)

Stained glass christmas trees, page 10
Use a rolling pin or meat mallet to gently tap and break up the lollies while they're still enclosed in their cellophane wrapping. Unwrap the lollies, separate the different colours into separate small bowls.

Cut out the Christmas tree shapes on baking paper, cut out the smaller shapes inside the trees, pull away the excess dough from the tree shapes. Slide the paper onto an oven tray. Use a skewer to make a hole in the top of each tree for the ribbon to be threaded through.

Bake the cookies for the suggested time, then sprinkle pieces of the crushed lollies into the cut-out centres, bake the cookies until they're firm to touch. Cool on the trays.

Jam wreaths, page 18
Brush around the edges of the rounds of dough with a tiny amount of water. Position the holly leaves around the edges of the rounds, overlapping each leaf slightly.

tips & techniques

Brush the leaves sparingly with water, sprinkle lightly with extra sugar. Spoon a little jam into the centres of the wreaths. Bake as directed.

Mini chocolate yule logs, page 38
To make four complete logs, cut four of the cakes in half crossways. Use a little ganache to join four pieces of the halved cakes to the ends of four whole cakes, to make longer logs.

Using the remaining four halved pieces of cake, trim a corner away, so the branch will sit snugly against the side of the log.

Join the cut pieces to the sides of the logs with a little ganache. You don't need the scraps of leftover cake for the log.

 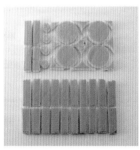  

Grating fresh coconut
Preheat oven to 220°C/200°C fan-forced. Using a strong metal skewer, pierce each "eye" of the coconut, drain away the milk. Place the coconut on an oven tray, roast for 10 minutes; cool. The coconut will split open itself (if it doesn't tap it firmly with a meat mallet or hammer) and the flesh will separate from the shell. Use a grater to grate the flesh.

Baby berry puddings, page 41
Cut one sponge crossways into ten 2cm slices, cut the slices in half. Cut two 2cm slices from the end of the remaining sponge, cut the slices in half. Cut four 2cm rounds and four 7cm rounds from the remaining sponge.

Line the pudding moulds generously with plastic wrap, leaving some overhanging the edges of the moulds. Place the small rounds of sponge into each mould, line the sides of each of the moulds with six pieces of sponge.

Rosy semi-freddo bombes, page 45
Using sharp scissors, cut out 12 x 16cm rounds from strong plastic, like the plastic used in resealable bags. Place the rounds on baking paper, spread the rounds with the melted white chocolate.

Drizzle teaspoons of the pink-tinted white chocolate randomly over the surface of the unset white chocolate.

Use a small metal spatula or blade of a table knife to swirl the chocolate for a marbled effect.

Remove the frozen ice cream bombes, one at a time, from the freezer, quickly drape the slightly firm chocolate-coated plastic, chocolate side-down, over each bombe. Quickly smooth the plastic with your hands, return the bombes to the freezer as you complete each one.

The coating will set quickly, in about 10 minutes. Peel the plastic away from the bombes, stand the bombes for 5 minutes before serving. The bombes can be frozen, without their plastic, for two days before serving, let them stand at room temperature for about 10 minutes before serving.

Making a paper piping bag
Cut a square of baking paper diagonally into two triangles. Hold the apex of the triangle towards you, then roll the paper into a cone shape, bringing the three points of the triangle together.

Staple the three points together, then fill the bag with chocolate, icing etc. Using sharp scissors, snip a tiny bit off the end of the bag, then test for the right sized opening by piping the chocolate. Snip off more of the tip if needed.

Roasting nuts
Roast nuts (including coconut) either on an oven tray in the oven at 180°C/160°C fan-forced, for about 5 minutes, or, in a heavy based pan, stirred constantly over a medium heat until evenly browned. Remove the nuts from the tray or pan to cool, as soon as they are browned.

Removing skin from hazelnuts
Roast hazelnuts on an oven tray in a 180°C/160°C fan-forced oven for about 5 minutes, or until browned lightly. Turn the nuts onto a clean tea towel, rub the nuts in the towel, most of the skins will come off the warm nuts.

Raspberry eggnog tartlets, page 46
Roll each portion of the pastry between sheets of baking paper large enough to fit into the 5cm x 10cm flan tins, ease the pastry down into the tins without stretching the pastry, trim the edges. Prick the bases well with a fork then refrigerate 30 minutes.

Line each tin with a strip of baking paper, fill the cavity of each tin with dried beans, peas or rice. Bake as directed.

Trio of jams – Citrus marmalade, page 62
Tie the reserved pith and seeds from the citrus fruit in a piece of muslin, tie into a bag securing with kitchen string. Add to the fruit mixture for overnight soaking. The seeds and pith contain pectin, which is necessary to set the jam.

To test if marmalade is ready, remove the pan from the heat, let the bubbles subside, drop a teaspoon of the marmalade onto a cold sauce, cool it in the fridge or freezer. Then, push the jam with your finger, if the marmalade is ready, a "skin" will have formed, and will wrinkle when the jam is pushed.

Pomegranate punch, page 73

Cut the ripe pomegranate in half crossways with a sharp knife. Hold one half of the pomegranate over a bowl, firmly tap the pomegranate on the skin with a wooden spoon, the seeds will fall out into the bowl.

Triple chocolate fudge, page 85

While the ingredients for the fudge are reaching the boil, place the candy thermometer in a small saucepan of cold water, then bring it to the boil. Place the now heated thermometer into the fudge to reach the correct temperature.

When the fudge has reached the correct temperature, remove the pan from the heat, leave the thermometer in the fudge until the temperature reduces to the correct temperature indicated in the recipe. Return the thermometer to the small pan of boiling water, remove from the heat, cool the thermometer in the water.

Use a wooden spoon to beat the fudge mixture for about 10 minutes, or until the fudge is smooth and satiny and will hold its shape when dropped from the spoon.

Truffle trio, page 57
Gold leaf can be bought from specialty kitchen and food stores. It needs to be handled gently and carefully. Apply the gold leaf to the truffles using a paint brush or tweezers, fragments of the gold leaf will break off as soon as it's touched, it is edible.

Mini christmas puddings, page 98
Drop the prepared pudding cloths into the boiler of boiling water. Using thick rubber gloves and tongs, remove one cloth at a time, wring out the excess water. Spread the cloth out on a flat surface and, working quickly, drop 2 tablespoons flour in the centre of the cloth; spread and rub the flour into an 18cm circle.

Gather the corners of the cloth together, pat and shape the pudding into a round shape. Tie the pudding securely and tightly around the cloth with kitchen string, as shown above. Leave two long loops of string to make handling the pudding easier.

If boiling one pudding (the best method if you have the time), tie the looped string to the handles of the boiler or large saucepan, so that the pudding is suspended in the boiling water. Cover the boiler with a tight-fitting lid and cook for the required time, replenishing the water as it evaporates.

glossary

almonds
blanched brown skins removed.
flaked paper-thin slices.
meal also called ground almonds.
slivered small lengthways-cut pieces.
baking powder a raising agent consisting two parts cream of tartar to one part bicarbonate of soda.
bicarbonate of soda also called baking soda.
blood orange a virtually seedless citrus fruit with blood-red-streaked rind and flesh; sweet, non-acidic, salmon-coloured pulp and juice wtih slight strawberry or raspberry overtones. The rind is not as bitter as an ordinary orange.
butter use salted or unsalted ('sweet') butter.
cachous small, round cake-decorating sweets available in silver, gold and various colours.
cardamom can be purchased in pod, seed or ground form. Has a distinctive aromatic, sweetly rich flavour.
chocolate
Bits also called chocolate chips and morsels. Hold their shape in baking.
dark eating made of cocoa liquor, cocoa butter and sugar.
milk eating most popular eating chocolate, mild and very sweet; similar in make-up to dark, but with the addition of milk solids.
white eating contains no cocoa solids, deriving its sweet flavour from cocoa butter. Is very sensitive to heat.
cinnamon available in pieces (called sticks or quills) and ground. The dried inner bark of the shoots of the Sri Lankan native cinnamon tree.
cloves can be used whole or in ground form. Has a strong scent and taste so should be used minimally.
cocoa powder also known as cocoa.
coconut
desiccated unsweetened and concentrated, dried finely shredded.
flaked dried flaked coconut flesh.
shredded thin strips of dried coconut flesh.
cointreau orange-flavoured liqueur.
cornflour also known as cornstarch.
cranberries available dried and frozen; have a rich, astringent flavour and used in sweet or savoury dishes.
cumquats orange-coloured citrus fruit about the size of walnuts. Usually preserved or used for making jam, the skin is always retained.
flour
plain an all-purpose wheat flour.

self-raising plain flour sifted with baking powder: 1 cup flour to 2 teaspoons baking powder.
gelatine (gelatin) we use powdered gelatine as a setting agent.
ginger
fresh also called green or root ginger; the thick gnarled root of a tropical plant. Can be kept, peeled, covered with dry sherry in a jar and refrigerated, or frozen in an airtight container.
glacé fresh ginger root preserved in sugar syrup.
glacé fruit fruit such as cherries, peaches, pineapple, orange and citron cooked in heavy sugar syrup then dried.
glucose syrup also known as liquid glucose; a sugary syrup made from starches such as wheat and corn.
gold leaf (edible) available from cake decorating or art supply stores.
grand marnier a brandy-based orange-flavoured liqueur.
macadamias native to Australia, a rich and buttery nut; store in the fridge because of its high oil content.
malibu a coconut-flavoured rum.
maple syrup distilled from the sap of maple trees found only in Canada and parts of North America. Maple-flavoured syrup is not an adequate substitute for the real thing.
marzipan a paste made from ground almonds, sugar and water. Similar to almond paste but sweeter, more pliable and finer in texture. Easily coloured and rolled to cover cakes or sculpted into shapes.
mixed spice a blend of ground spices usually consisting of cinnamon, allspice and nutmeg.
nutmeg dried nut of an evergreen tree; available in ground form or you can grate your own with a fine grater.
orange flower water concentrated flavouring made from orange blossoms.
pomegranate dark-red, leathery-skinned fresh fruit about the size of an orange filled with hundreds of seeds, each wrapped in an edible lucent-crimson pulp having a unique tangy sweet-sour flavour.
ready-made almond icing available from supermarkets etc. You can use marzipan instead of the almond-paste.
ready-made white icing also called soft icing, ready-to-roll and prepared fondant.
rice paper there are two products sold as rice paper. Banh trang (made from rice flour and water) is dipped

briefly in water, to become pliable wrappers for food. The other, edible, translucent glossy rice paper is made from a dough of water combined with the pith of an Asian shrub called the rice-paper plant. Resembling a grainy sheet of paper and whiter than banh trang, it is imported from Holland. Use in confectionery making and baking; never eat it uncooked.
rosewater extract made from crushed rose petals, called gulab in India; used for its aromatic quality.
star anise a dried star-shaped pod whose seeds have an astringent aniseed flavour; commonly used to flavour stocks and marinades.
sugar
brown a soft, fine granulated sugar containing molasses to give its characteristic colour.
caster also called superfine or finely granulated table sugar.
crystals its sugar grains are coarser than granulated table (crystal) sugar; available from specialty food stores.
icing also known as confectioners' sugar or powdered sugar; crushed granulated sugar with added cornflour (about 3 per cent).
muscovado a fine-grained, moist sugar that comes in two types: light and dark. Light muscovado has a light toffee flavour, and is good for sticky toffee sauce and caramel ice-cream. Dark muscovado is used in sweet and spicy sauces.
palm also known as nam tan pip, jaggery, jawa or gula melaka; made from the sap of the sugar palm tree. Light brown to black in colour and usually sold in rock-hard cakes; use brown sugar if hard to find.
pure icing also called confectioners' sugar or powdered sugar.
white coarse and granulated; also known as table sugar.
tamarind the tamarind tree produces clusters of hairy brown pods, each of which is filled with seeds and a viscous pulp, that are dried and pressed into the blocks of tamarind found in Asian food shops. Releases a sweet-sour, slightly astringent taste.
treacle thick, dark syrup not unlike molasses.
vanilla bean dried long, thin pod from a tropical golden orchid grown in central and South America and Tahiti; the minuscule black seeds inside the bean are used to impart a distinctively sweet vanilla flavour.

conversion chart

measures

One Australian metric measuring cup holds approximately 250ml; one Australian metric tablespoon holds 20ml; one Australian metric teaspoon holds 5ml.

The difference between one country's measuring cups and another's is within a two- or three-teaspoon variance, and will not affect your cooking results. North America, New Zealand and the United Kingdom use a 15ml tablespoon.

All cup and spoon measurements are level. The most accurate way of measuring dry ingredients is to weigh them. When measuring liquids, use a clear glass or plastic jug with the metric markings.

We use large eggs with an average weight of 60g.

dry measures

METRIC	IMPERIAL
15g	½oz
30g	1oz
60g	2oz
90g	3oz
125g	4oz (¼lb)
155g	5oz
185g	6oz
220g	7oz
250g	8oz (½lb)
280g	9oz
315g	10oz
345g	11oz
375g	12oz (¾lb)
410g	13oz
440g	14oz
470g	15oz
500g	16oz (1lb)
750g	24oz (1½lb)
1kg	32oz (2lb)

liquid measures

METRIC	IMPERIAL
30ml	1 fluid oz
60ml	2 fluid oz
100ml	3 fluid oz
125ml	4 fluid oz
150ml	5 fluid oz (¼ pint/1 gill)
190ml	6 fluid oz
250ml	8 fluid oz
300ml	10 fluid oz (½ pint)
500ml	16 fluid oz
600ml	20 fluid oz (1 pint)
1000ml (1 litre)	1¾ pints

length measures

3mm	⅛in
6mm	¼in
1cm	½in
2cm	¾in
2.5cm	1in
5cm	2in
6cm	2½in
8cm	3in
10cm	4in
13cm	5in
15cm	6in
18cm	7in
20cm	8in
23cm	9in
25cm	10in
28cm	11in
30cm	12in (1ft)

oven temperatures

These oven temperatures are only a guide for conventional ovens. For fan-forced ovens, check the manufacturer's manual.

	°C (CELSIUS)	°F (FAHRENHEIT)	GAS MARK
Very slow	120	250	½
Slow	150	275-300	1-2
Moderately slow	160	325	3
Moderate	180	350-375	4-5
Moderately hot	200	400	6
Hot	220	425-450	7-8
Very hot	240	475	9

index

ARE YOU MISSING SOME OF THE WORLD'S FAVOURITE COOKBOOKS?

The Australian Women's Weekly Cookbooks are available from bookshops, cookshops, supermarkets and other stores all over the world. You can also buy direct from the publisher, using the order form below.

To order: Mail or fax – photocopy or complete the order form above, and send your credit card details or cheque payable to: Australian Consolidated Press (UK), ACP Books, 10 Scirocco Close, Moulton Park Office Village, Northampton NN3 6AP
phone (+44) (0)1604 642 200
fax (+44) (0)1604 642 300
email books@acpuk.com
or order online at www.acpuk.com
Non-UK residents: We accept the credit cards listed on the coupon, or cheques, drafts or International Money Orders payable in sterling and drawn on a UK bank. Credit card charges are at the exchange rate current at the time of payment.
Postage and packing UK: Add £1.00 per order plus £1.75 per book.
Postage and packing overseas: Add £2.00 per order plus £3.50 per book.
All pricing current at time of going to press and subject to change/availability.
Offer ends 31.12.2008

TITLE	RRP	QTY
100 Fast Fillets	£6.99	
A Taste of Chocolate	£6.99	
After Work Fast	£6.99	
Beginners Cooking Class	£6.99	
Beginners Simple Meals	£6.99	
Beginners Thai	£6.99	
Best Food Fast	£6.99	
Breads & Muffins	£6.99	
Brunches, Lunches & Treats	£6.99	
Cafe Classics	£6.99	
Cafe Favourites	£6.99	
Cakes Bakes & Desserts	£6.99	
Cakes Biscuits & Slices	£6.99	
Cakes Cooking Class	£6.99	
Caribbean Cooking	£6.99	
Casseroles	£6.99	
Casseroles & Slow-Cooked Classics	£6.99	
Cheap Eats	£6.99	
Cheesecakes: baked and chilled	£6.99	
Chicken	£6.99	
Chinese and the foods of Thailand, Vietnam, Malaysia & Japan	£6.99	
Chinese Cooking Class	£6.99	
Chocs & Treats	£6.99	
Cookies & Biscuits	£6.99	
Cooking Class Cake Decorating	£6.99	
Cupcakes & Fairycakes	£6.99	
Detox	£6.99	
Dinner Lamb	£6.99	
Dinner Seafood	£6.99	
Easy Comfort Food	£6.99	
Easy Curry	£6.99	
Easy Midweek Meals	£6.99	
Easy Spanish-Style	£6.99	
Food for Fit and Healthy Kids	£6.99	
Foods of the Mediterranean	£6.99	
Foods That Fight Back	£6.99	
Fresh Food Fast	£6.99	
Fresh Food for Babies & Toddlers	£6.99	
Good Food for Babies & Toddlers	£6.99	
Great Kids' Cakes	£6.99	
Greek Cooking Class	£6.99	
Grills	£6.99	
Healthy Heart Cookbook	£6.99	
Indian Cooking Class	£6.99	
Japanese Cooking Class	£6.99	

TITLE	RRP	QTY
Just For One	£6.99	
Just For Two	£6.99	
Kids' Birthday Cakes	£6.99	
Kids Cooking	£6.99	
Kids' Cooking Step-by-Step	£6.99	
Low-carb, Low-fat	£6.99	
Low-fat Food for Life	£6.99	
Low-fat Meals in Minutes	£6.99	
Main Course Salads	£6.99	
Mexican	£6.99	
Middle Eastern Cooking Class	£6.99	
Midweek Meals in Minutes	£6.99	
Mince in Minutes	£6.99	
Mini Bakes	£6.99	
Moroccan & the Foods of North Africa	£6.99	
Muffins, Scones & Breads	£6.99	
New Casseroles	£6.99	
New Curries	£6.99	
New French Food	£6.99	
New Salads	£6.99	
One Pot	£6.99	
Party Food and Drink	£6.99	
Pasta Meals in Minutes	£6.99	
Quick & Simple Cooking	£6.99	
Rice & Risotto	£6.99	
Saucery	£6.99	
Sauces Salsas & Dressings	£6.99	
Sensational Stir-Fries	£6.99	
Simple Healthy Meals	£6.99	
Simple Starters Mains & Puds	£6.99	
Slim	£6.99	
Soup	£6.99	
Stir-fry	£6.99	
Superfoods for Exam Success	£6.99	
Tapas Mezze Antipasto & other bites	£6.99	
Thai Cooking Class	£6.99	
Traditional Italian	£6.99	
Vegetarian Meals in Minutes	£6.99	
Vegie Food	£6.99	
Vegie Stars	£6.99	
Wicked Sweet Indulgences	£6.99	
Wok Meals in Minutes	£6.99	
TOTAL COST	£	

Mr/Mrs/Ms _____

Address _____

_____ Postcode _____

Day time phone _____ email* (optional) _____

I enclose my cheque/money order for £ _____

or please charge £ _____

to my: ☐ Access   ☐ Mastercard   ☐ Visa   ☐ Diners Club

Card number | | | | | | | | | | | | | | | | |

Expiry date _____ 3 digit security code *(found on reverse of card)* _____

Cardholder's name_____ Signature _____

* By including your email address, you consent to receipt of any email regarding this magazine, and other emails which inform you of ACP's other publications, products, services and events, and to promote third party goods and services you may be interested in.

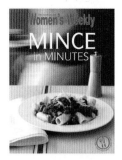

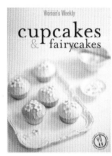
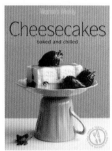

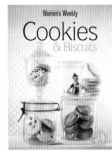

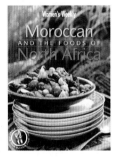

You'll find these books and more available on sale at bookshops, cookshops, selected supermarkets or direct from the publisher (see order form page 119).

TEST KITCHEN
Food director Pamela Clark
Associate food editor Alexandra Somerville
Home economist Cathie Lonnie

ACP BOOKS
General manager Christine Whiston
Editorial director Susan Tomnay
Creative director Hieu Chi Nguyen
Senior editor Stephanie Kistner
Designer Hannah Blackmore
Director of sales Brian Cearnes
Marketing manager Bridget Cody
Business analyst Rebecca Varela
Operations manager David Scotto
Production manager Victoria Jefferys
International rights enquiries Laura Bamford
lbamford@acpuk.com

acp books

ACP Books are published by ACP Magazines
a division of PBL Media Pty Limited
Group publisher, Women's lifestyle
Pat Ingram
Director of sales, Women's lifestyle
Lynette Phillips
Commercial manager, Women's lifestyle
Seymour Cohen
Marketing director, Women's lifestyle
Matthew Dominello
Public relations manager, Women's lifestyle
Hannah Deveraux
Creative director, Events, Women's lifestyle
Luke Bonnano
Research Director, Women's lifestyle
Justin Stone
ACP Magazines, Chief Executive officer
Scott Lorson
PBL Media, Chief Executive officer
Ian Law

Produced by ACP Books, Sydney.
Published by ACP Books, a division of
ACP Magazines Ltd, 54 Park St, Sydney;
GPO Box 4088, Sydney, NSW 2001.
phone (02) 9282 8618 fax (02) 9267 9438.
acpbooks@acpmagazines.com.au
www.acpbooks.com.au
Printed by Dai Nippon in Korea.

Australia Distributed by Network Services,
phone +61 2 9282 8777 fax +61 2 9264 3278
networkweb@networkservicescompany.com.au
United Kingdom Distributed by Australian
Consolidated Press (UK),
phone (01604) 642 200 fax (01604) 642 300
books@acpuk.com
New Zealand Distributed by Netlink
Distribution Company,
phone (9) 366 9966 ask@ndc.co.nz
South Africa Distributed by PSD Promotions,
phone (27 11) 392 6065/6/7
fax (27 11) 392 6079/80
orders@psdprom.co.za
Canada Distributed by Publishers Group Canada
phone (800) 663 5714 fax (800) 565 3770
service@raincoast.com

A catalogue record for this book is available from
the British Library.
ISBN 978-1-86396-776-1
© ACP Magazines Ltd 2008
ABN 18 053 273 546
This publication is copyright. No part of it may be
reproduced or transmitted in any form without the
written permission of the publishers.
Scanpan cookware is used in the AWW Test Kitchen.
Send recipe enquiries to
askpamela@acpmagazines.com.au